Stories of ...lay ...gs

The Story of
BALLOONS

by Mae Respicio

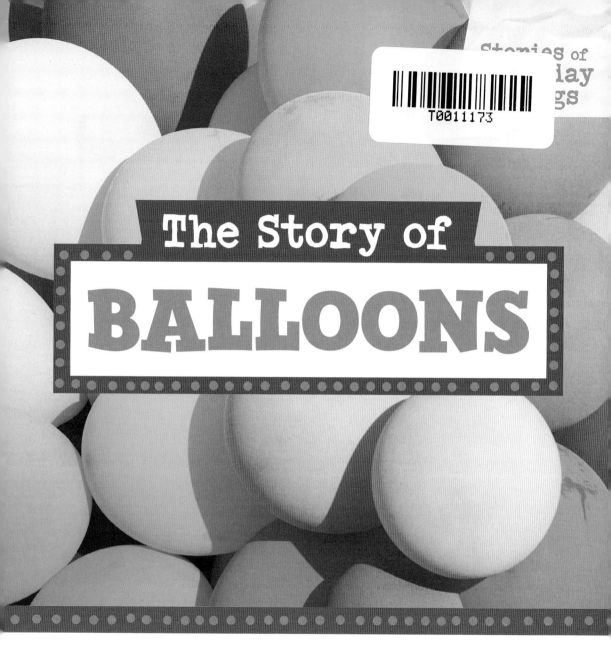

PEBBLE
a capstone imprint

Published by Pebble, an imprint of Capstone
1710 Roe Crest Drive, North Mankato, Minnesota 56003
capstonepub.com

Library of Congress Cataloging-in-Publication Data
is available on the Library of Congress website.
ISBN: 9780756577452 (hardcover)
ISBN: 9780756577575 (paperback)
ISBN: 9780756577513 (ebook PDF)

Summary: Discover fun facts about balloons that you can
share at your next party in this fact-filled book.

Editorial Credits
Editor: Christianne Jones; Designer: Jaime Willems;
Media Researcher: Rebekah Hubstenberger; Production
Specialist: Whitney Schaefer

Image Credits
Alamy: Heritage Image Partnership Ltd, 12; Getty Images:
boonchai wedmakawand, 24, duncan1890, 10, Eric
VANDEVILLE/Gamma-Rapho, 17, Granger Wootz, 13,
Hulton Archive, 9, IAN BODDY/SPL, 19, Cover (back),
iStock/DKart, 1, kali9, 25, Three Lions, 11; NASA: Goddard
Space Flight Center, 27, Kim Shiflett, 26; Shutterstock:
Africa Studio, Cover (front, balloons), bluehand, Cover
(front, dog balloon), Jaromir Chalabala, 15, Kattiya.L, 16,
18, 21, KlingSup, 28, pics five, 5, www.hollandfoto.net,
23; The Metropolitan Museum of Art, New York: The Elisha
Whittelsey Collection, The Elisha Whittelsey Fund, 1968, 7

Design Elements: Luria, Pooretat moonsana

All internet sites appearing in back matter were available
and accurate when this book was sent to press.

Table of Contents

Words in bold appear in the glossary.

Early Balloons

They're bright. They're bouncy. They float. They pop. We're talking about balloons!

Balloons come in all shapes and sizes. They help people celebrate. They make people smile. They can even carry people through the sky! But how did balloons come to be?

The earliest balloons were made from animal bladders. They were first dried out. Then they were filled with air. In the 1300s, the Aztecs made balloon sculptures from cat **intestines**. They were presented as sacrifices to the Aztec gods.

Most balloons today are made from latex, mylar, and foil. They're usually filled with gas such as helium, oxygen, or air. Balloons can also be filled with water.

A child blows up an animal bladder.

How Balloons Were Born

Michael Faraday was a professor in London. In 1824, he had an idea. He put together two round, rubber sheets. The sheets were coated inside with flour. This kept them from sticking together.

Faraday then sealed the sheets. He filled the middle with hydrogen gas. What happened? It rose! It was the first rubber balloon.

Michael Faraday

Thomas Hancock

A year later, British businessman Thomas Hancock sold balloon kits. He also created a balloon-making process using molds. Before long, people began using balloons at parties.

In 1839, Charles Goodyear made a new type of rubber. J.G. Ingram in London designed a balloon **prototype** in 1847. It was made from the new rubber. Eventually, it became the toy balloon we know today.

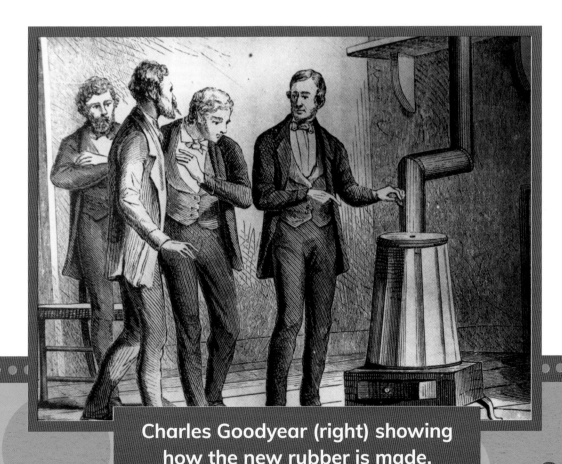

Charles Goodyear (right) showing how the new rubber is made.

Round, rubber balloons were first made in the United States around 1907. They became very popular.

The first non-round balloons were made in 1912. They looked like long noodles. People began twisting these balloons into shapes in the 1930s.

A man makes balloon animals in London, England, in 1966.

The first foil balloons were made in the 1970s. They had messages printed on them. They said things like, "Happy Birthday!"

How Balloons Are Made Today

Today, latex balloons are the most common. Did you know that latex comes from trees? Rubber trees, in fact. The trees have a milky white sap in their bark. This is natural liquid latex. The rubber tree is native to South America. Today, most rubber tree farms are in Asia.

Synthetic latex is also used to make balloons. It is made in factories using chemicals.

Natural liquid latex from a rubber tree

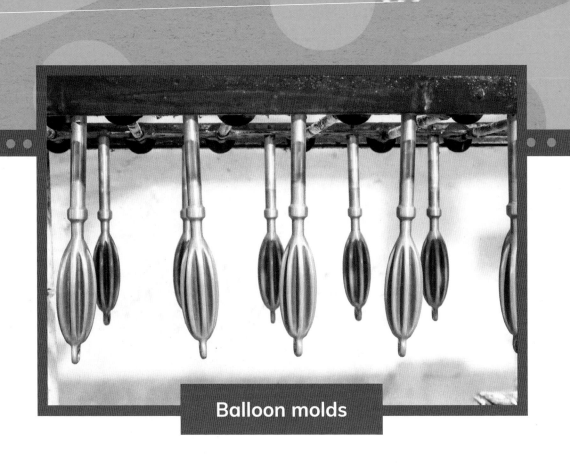

Balloon molds

How do so many balloons get made? By using machines and molds. Metal molds are shaped like a deflated balloon. Big machines take the molds and move them through lots of steps.

First, liquid latex is dyed in different colors. The colors are mixed in huge tanks. You wouldn't want balloons to be all the same color, would you?

Dyed latex tank

Next, the molds get heated. Then they're dipped in calcium nitrate. This chemical coating attracts the latex. Have you seen white powder inside a balloon? This is where it comes from. Finally, the molds are dipped into the dyed latex.

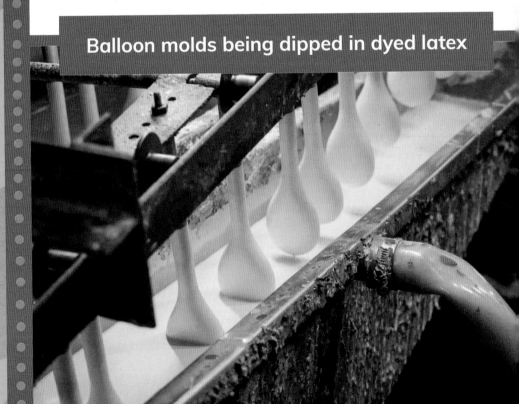

Balloon molds being dipped in dyed latex

Balloons drying after being dipped

After the balloons dry, they get brushed. This rolls up the bottoms. It creates the lip you blow on to fill a balloon.

Are the balloons done yet? Almost! Next, machines pull the balloons off the molds. Then they are washed and checked. Factory workers look for **defects**.

Computers also help control the quality of the balloons. They control things such as oven temperatures. Once a batch of balloons is ready, they are packaged.

Now are the balloons done? Yes! But they still have to be **distributed** around the world.

How Balloons Reach Us

Balloons are big business! They are often made and shipped in large numbers. Many businesses sell balloons. Street merchants and large party shops sell them. So do gift shops and online stores. You can even find them in grocery stores!

Where do these balloons come from? Businesses get their supplies from a balloon distributor.

Balloon distributors are businesses too. They work with factories around the world. In the United States, suppliers sell about 3 billion balloons each year!

The boxes of balloons get shipped from the factories to warehouses by **freight carriers**. If they are going a long way, they can get shipped by airplane.

Giant warehouses store the boxes until they are ready to be delivered. Trucks deliver them from the warehouses to stores.

Are balloons good only for parties? No! They're used in several ways. Medical balloons can help unblock **arteries**. Researchers use large balloons to help check weather conditions. NASA uses balloons to lift things into space.

Weather balloon

NASA balloon

Balloons are a lot of fun. And they can be very useful. They're one of many everyday things used in our everyday lives.

Keep it Up!

• • • • • • • • • • • • • • • • • • • •

Balloons can be used for learning, decorating, and playing. This fun balloon game can be played inside or outside.

What you need:

- an inflated balloon
- at least three people
- a timer

What you do:

1. Have everyone stand in a circle and hold hands.

2. The goal is to keep the balloon in the air while holding hands.

3. Start the timer.

4. Work together to keep the balloon in the air. Use your feet, elbows, chest, head, or the backs of your hands.

5. When the balloon drops, start over.

6. Try to beat your best time every round.

GLOSSARY

artery (AR-tuh-ree)—a tube that carries blood away from the heart to all parts of the body

defect (DEE-fekt)—an imperfection

distribute (di-STRI-yoot)—to deliver products to various places

freight carrier (FRAYT-KAR-ee-er)—a person or company that ships goods from one place to another

intestine (in-TESS-tin)—a long tube below the stomach that digests food

prototype (PROH-tuh-type)—the first version of an invention that tests an idea to see if it will work

synthetic (sin-THET-ik)—something that is made by people rather than found in nature

READ MORE

Gerencer, Thomas. *How It's Made: The Creation of Everyday Items.* Abrams Books for Young Readers, 2022.

Giovinco, Gerry. *The Big Book of Balloon Art.* Mineola, NY: Dover Publications, 2019.

Shores, Lori. *How to Make a Mystery Smell Balloon.* Mankato, MN: Capstone, 2018.

INTERNET SITES

Kidadl: 51 Astonishing and Fun Balloon Facts You Probably Didn't Know!
kidadl.com/facts/astonishing-and-fun-balloon-facts-you-probably-didn-t-know

Kiddle: Balloon Facts for Kids
kids.kiddle.co/Balloon

National Weather Service: Weather Balloons
weather.gov/bmx/kidscorner_weatherballoons

INDEX

ABOUT THE AUTHOR

Mae Respicio is a nonfiction writer and middle grade author whose novel, *The House That Lou Built*, won an Asian/Pacific American Libraries Association Honor Award and was an NPR Best Book. Mae lives with her family in California and some of her favorite everyday things include books, beaches, and ube ice cream.